# High School Dropout

## The teens guide for staying in school

ISBN-13: 978-1497500044

ISBN-10: 1497500044

# INTRODUCTION

Every 26 seconds in America a teen drops out of high school, that's 1.3 million a year. In this book teens will discover that getting an education and staying in school is the foundation for their futures.

Helping them understand the importance of the opportunity to excel in school by learning and earning good grades will prepare them for life and the market place. We are affected by what we know, so you can't be lazy in learning.

# Foreword

Raymond Shinault has a passion for youth, he has a passion for helping them understand how important they are to themselves and to the future. Many times we lack vision in life, we just can't see how we are going to make it but when we experience the infusion of confidence and belief through the eyes of someone else it somehow seems possible. Let Raymond Shinault's vision show you how it is possible. The cure 4 your life starts with you!

Sir Charles Cary, Alternative Recourse Expert
National Trainer, Speaker & Author

# Contents

# Chapter 1

## We have a problem in America

### Students are dropping out

Every 26 seconds someone drops out of High School Resulting in over 1.3 Million High School Students Dropping out in this country every year. "If you drop out of high school, how many good jobs are out there for you? None. Increasing the graduation rate and reducing the dropout rate are important because those numbers are directly tied to the nation's economy. The dropout rate was highest among high school seniors who are males. Nearly 1 in 5 U.S men between 16 and 24 were dropouts. Studies show dropouts earn 41% less than high-school graduates and are much more likely to be unemployed, on public assistance or imprisoned all at the taxpayers' expense. The dropout rate has long been a priority on national policy agendas. President Barack Obama's administration alone has spent billions in federal grant programs to improve graduation rates and reduce dropout rates. Although the drop out rates in America have been steadily declining over the 2000s, there's still much reason for concern, especially about the ethnic and racial disparities revealed by dropout statistics. The level of education an individual reaches is often a great predictor of future career and life achievement. Those who drop out of high school, or even college, tend to face more struggles than those with a solid education. In it's report the CFR's Renewing America initiative, found that the United States has fallen 10 spots in both high school and college graduation rates in the last 30 years. Research has shown that poor academic achievement is one of the strongest predictors of becoming a high school dropout.

  Poor academic achievement has a very strong relationship with increased likelihood of dropping out. Grade retention can increase the odds of dropping out by as much as 250 percent above those of similar students who were not retained. Students who drop out typically have a history of absenteeism, grade retention and academic trouble and are more disengaged from school life. While the above factors certainly place a student at risk for dropout, they are not always the reason the student identifies as their motivation for dropping out. One study found that the main reasons students reported for dropping out included uninteresting classes. The current unemployment rate for high school dropouts is about 56 percent greater than that for high school graduates.

Lifetime earnings for this group are estimated to be $260,000 less than those for high school graduates. Female dropouts are much more likely to become single mothers and consequently be more likely to have an income under the poverty threshold or live on welfare. High school dropouts make up 68 percent of the nation's prison population. Additionally, high school dropouts have a life expectancy that is 3–5 years shorter than high school graduates. High school dropouts affect our economy and the social well being of our nation. For each cohort of 18-year-olds who never complete high school, the U.S. loses $192 billion in income and tax revenue. Because of these factors, an average high school dropout will cost the government over $292,000. Families, schools, and communities influence students' decisions to drop out in several ways. For example, students living with both parents have lower dropout rates and higher graduation rates compared to students in other living arrangements. The employment status of their parents incomes play roles, as do parenting practices. These include monitoring a child's progress in school, communicating with the school, and knowing the parents of their children's friends. Students also are more likely to drop out if they have a sibling who did so (Rumberger and Lim, 2008).

Enough about all of the statistics. When students drop out of school, the course of their lives will be drastically affected. Your education, knowledge, skills and experience all are investments in your ability to contribute a value for which you can be paid. But they are like any other investments. They are highly speculative. Getting an education is in your own best interest. You can reap massive benefits for doing so. But reap stiff consequences for not doing so. Take getting your education very seriously. One of the things that all successful students have in common, is that they've conquered the temptation to give up and Quit! Students make the decision to start pursuing your goals and dreams now. Why? Because it's a huge step. Learn how to become the best possible person you can be. Learn how to make the best of your talents and opportunities. Learn how to deal with problems in positive ways. Learn how to face what ever life brings. Learn the things you must learn to make continued positive progress year after year. 19 out of 20 people quit before they reach their intended goal. If you want to reach your goals in life you must never ever QUIT! Dropping out of school cannot become an option for you to take if you want to become success in life, and the market place. Learn to use the ant philosophy. Ants never Quit! For if you stop him, he will start looking for another way. How long will he look? He will look until he finds it or until he dies. 1.3 Million of you are dropping out of our High Schools in this country every single year. If a High School dropout fills out an application, and a High School graduate fills out that same application. Who? Will get the job.

It will be the graduate. Why? Because they have earned their High School diploma. Receiving an education prepares you for the market place. Remember this" Preparation is never wasted time. Do what is necessary and not what is popular. Do what you have to as quick as you can. Why? So that you can do what you want to for as long as you can. Life is like mathematics. We all want to have the right answer at the end but for that to happen we need to know what to add, where to subtract, how to multiply and when to divide. A small mistake can lead not only to an unexpected answer but also will not give you a chance to undo the wrong step. So we need to be careful while solving our mathematics called life. Teens if your going to be a success in life you will have to work for it. Success does not come from thin air. It comes from getting started. You have to begin or you will never have it. Hard Work and Dedication is what you will have to commit to in order to graduate. Wrong choices repeated over time will take you down and out. Right choices repeated over time will take you upward and onward to your success. Success defines the potential in you." Be your own person because no one can take that away from you. No one is ever going to be you." Be very careful with the choices you make in life. For there are adults all over the United States who are still trying to undo some of the things they did when they were your age. There are consequences for the choices we make.

What limits you from achieving success in school or in life is never circumstances or fate. The limiting factor is always you and what you believe. If you can believe it you can achieve it! Remember this if it were not possible to fail, it would not be possible to succeed. So learn all that you can learn and become smarter than you are right now. For information will change your situation once you apply it to your life. Success is something that you attract, by the person you become. It's not something that you pursue, chase or run after. By developing yourself into an attractive valuable person you attract success. Remember it all starts with getting an education. The person that you become is much more valuable than what you get. There are numerous possibilities available for you to become the best possible version of your unique self.

Life gives all of us an opportunity to excel at everything we do, everything that peaks our interest. We need to work to be the best possible versions of ourselves daily! I want you to look at yourself and see your unique strengths, abilities, experience and unlimited potential, as tools to begin and sustain your journey, toward the future that you desire. How ever you define success. Operating at your full-potential basically means doing the right things at the right times. That's where it all starts, and that takes alot of courage. When you start living your full-potential you will gain the courage and faith to make the right choices, resulting in having that success. There is no such thing as a lucky break. No one has ever become successful in school or in life by accident. If you are going to be successful in school or life, you will have to do it on purpose. How? By taking small steps everyday toward that success and the goals you set for yourself. Don't be afraid to fail for it is the secret to your success. Failure teaches us what not to do, it is a education with in itself. The more you learn and apply those things you've learned the closer you get to success. Be serious about your on going education, Do your best to get it all. The knowledge that you will gain from intense study, will serve you well throughout your life. It's not about the family you come from. It's not about the school you come from nor city. It's not about good looks or good luck. There's only one difference between the teen's that are successful and those who are not. They never entertain the thought of dropping out of school and simply Quit on themselves and their dream! You can't control your circumstances. What you can control is how you react to your circumstances, and how you feel about yourself. Students on the success curve are pulled by the future, while students who dwell on the failure curve are pulled by the past. Don't worry about the people in your past; there's a reason they didn't make it into your future."Young people these days will do anything to be accepted by their so called friends, that they don't realize what they do can and will affect their futures immensely. Your attitude determines both their simplest and most complicated actions, from the way you carry yourselves, to the way you deal with hard times. We all know attitude is everything Why? because it determines the quality of your life. Never tell someone that you will do something, within a certain time frame and then not do it. Become a person of your word. You really have no excuse as to why you are not putting forth the effort to living up to your full-potential in school or in life. Take full responsibility for what happens to you. It's one of the highest forms of human maturity, excepting full responsibility. This will be the day that you have past from childhood to adulthood. The day you except full responsibility. If you want something get up and go get it. You have to start with a plan. But the plan you begin with will not be the plan that gets you there. Your plan will have to change over and over again. For you will meet obstacles, the unexpected will happen. You will have to adjust course for you will be continually learning. You may say why bother if my plan isn't going to get me there, why make one in the first place. Because the plan gives you a place to begin. Without it your dream will never become reality. When you do the small, positive things, it increases the chances that other positive things will happen for you. Your smallest actions affect you and the people around you, even when you don't see it or aren't aware of it. Graduating high school is the beginning of your successful future commit to hard work and dedication and make it happen and you will be glad you did.

# Chapter 2

# Education is Important

## Why do Students Quit School

For some teen students it's not cool to be a success in school. If you do well others will tease you. Failure is cool to these students. It's cool not to do your very best.

Do not believe these students for if you do, you will set into motion a tendency for failure throughout your entire life. If you exercise for a couple of days you won't notice much difference. But after a couple of months you will notice a big difference. If you read 10 pages of a good book everyday it might not seem like much. But after one year reading 10 pages everyday, you will have read more than two dozen 150 page books. Just a little bit done everyday will result into huge rewards over time. Like anything else, when it comes to goals, we tend to see things like they're on the big screen, but they're not. Though your dreams may be big, remember that the steps you're taking to get there are HUGE!!!!!!!! The average income of a High School dropout is $18.343 per yr. if they can find a job.

For High School Graduates it's $27.963. When it comes to our ethic groups Latino and African American's and native American's 50% of them won't graduate. Dropouts cost our tax payers 8 Billion dollars every year, for public assistant programs like food stamps and welfare. We send more kids to prison than we do to college. Approximately half of all dropouts ages 16 to 24 are unemployed 14.7 % to be exact. Statistics shows that only 1 out of 3 high school students will graduate high school. There's been no Community that has escape this dropout rate epidemic. If you Quit school you are making the biggest mistake of your life. Dropping out of high school is something that know student should ever do. The Oklahoma Senate Education Committee approved a bill that prohibits students under the age of 18 from dropping out of school. Some students allow friends or peer pressure from other high school drop outs, family or other outside relationships impact their decision to drop out of school. This also encompasses teens who opt to drop out high school to join a gang or to be accepted in other teen groups and street communities. One of the biggest reasons a teen will drop out of high school is because they simply lack interest in gaining an education. Out of 10,000 public high school drop outs, 7,000 of them confessed to their lack of interest to complete high school.

In the past, teen pregnancy accounted for 15% of the high school drop out rate among teens between the ages of 15 - 18. However, these numbers have sharply declined to about 4% on the average.

A number of public schools have opted to reform the school to cater to pregnant teens. Some states have high schools specifically for pregnant teens and teen mothers to ensure they complete high school in an environment that does not judge them or discount the impact or significance of their circumstance. Dropping out of high school is due to the high school students perception of an alternative lifestyle in which education does not play an important role.

A common reason why teens dropout of school is because they have been introduced to drug dealing or some other illegal way of earning money.

These students may view high school as a waste of time because they don't need an education to sell drugs or any illegal way of earning money for that matter. But the major problem with this is my mentor said" If someone is going down the wrong road, he doesn't need motivation to speed him up. What he needs is education to turn him around." 21% of high school seniors say they get high and 41% of the same group report drinking alcohol. These students are literally moving around in an intoxicated daze. Immature behavior is then amplified due to being under the influence. Drunk driving, poor grades and attendance, anti-social and violent behavior and the list goes on. Drinking alcohol and taking drugs destroys lives. I want to warn you to never start drinking or taking drugs at all ,for it will affect your future and the life you live. For the things that we do to ourselves not only affect us it affects the people who love us. It will also keep you from living up to their full potential. One of the greatest motivating factors to a better life, are these powerful words. I don't want to live like this anymore. We all must commit to life long learning. So get all the information you can while in school and apply those things in your life. Then watch great things happen for you. Statistics show that 55% of the nation's students between the ages of 15 and 19 will successfully complete high school and receive their high school diploma. Another 15% will receive their GED or high school equivalency before the age of 24, which accounts for 70% of those students that will graduate annually. The remaining 30% of high school students will drop out of school before reaching the 12th grade. Research has indicated that success in middle school is a strong indicator for success in high school.

You are affected by what you know. So don't be lazy in learning. You are also affected by what you feel. What you feel about your past can affect your attitude. It's important to make the past useful. Past failures as well as successes can help you better your life only if you learn from them.

My mentor Jim Rohn said" "Learning is the beginning of wealth. Learning is the beginning of health.

Learning is the beginning of spirituality. Searching and learning is where the miracle process all begins. You can create a better future by spending less time in the past and taking action in the present. If you find yourself creating a habit of quitting it will follow you throughout your life. Habits controls our lives and we often take habits for granted. We seldom realize the enormous power they have over us. That power lies in whether or not those habits are positive or negative. Your habits extend into all areas of your life. By creating positive habits you allow yourself a platform for success in all you do. If you want to know your past, look into your present conditions. If you want to know your future, look into your present actions." It is not the broken dream that breaks your heart but the dream you didn't dare to dream." Starting from today, dream as BIG as you want to, dream without putting limits on that dream, because there is nothing impossible if you will only BELIEVE. Teenagers are to blame for the enormous dropout rate. For their lack integrity, and the fact they are not willing to work hard enough to be successful. Students should take full responsibility for the actions they cause, not blame other people for troubles, because it's your life not theirs. So many people are saying that it's the parents fault or the teachers fault or the schools fault that students dropout of school. Its not the parents fault they just want the best for their young person and sometimes forget that their child is between child hood and adult hood. You will need ideas and goals to plan for your future. Don't forget inspiration for you will need it to succeed. Dropping out is defined as leaving school without a high school diploma or equivalent credential such as a General Educational Development (GED) certificate as defined by the National Center for Education Statistics. It's been known for years that young people who do not earn a high school diploma face many more problems later in life than people who graduate. Dropouts are more likely to be unemployed, have poor health, live in poverty, be on public assistance, and become single parents. If you're spending your life in search of a worthy goal and it's something you want to do, please graduate high school first. Then follow your dream and make it a reality! There are no short cuts to success in life. There is a worthy process for doing what you want to do and accomplish what you want to accomplish. Graduating high school is just a part of the process of achievement of a better life and better future. Some of the reasons students give for dropping of out school, are they didn't like school in general or the school they were attending. Were failing, getting poor grades, or couldn't keep up with school work. Didn't get along with teachers and/or students. Had disciplinary problems, were suspended, or expelled didn't feel safe in school. Got a job, had a family to support, or had trouble managing both school and work. Got married, got pregnant, or became a parent or had a drug or alcohol problem. Here's another way to learn and it's from other people. Learn from what you see that means pay attention. Success leaves clues. If you would be a better observer of the winners and the losers those who are doing well and those who are falling behind. Take good mental notes and adjust what your doing based on what you see. "

There are some things in life you know you shouldn't do, but you are so caught up in the high maintenance society and its demands that you completely forget that everything you do will have its consequence. Because high school completion has become a basic prerequisite for many entry-level jobs, as well as higher education, the economic consequences of leaving high school without a diploma are severe.

On average, dropouts are more likely to be unemployed than high school graduates and to earn less money when they eventually secure work. One national study noted that dropouts comprise nearly half of the heads of households on welfare.

Employed dropouts in a variety of studies reported working at unskilled jobs or at low-paying service occupations offering little opportunity for advancement.

Many employers will only hire applicants with at least a high school diploma. Youth crime, gang involvement and violence are additional reasons students drop out. The New York Times said that approximately one tenth of teen males who have dropped out are in jail or prison on any given day. The percentage is higher for young black male dropouts at a startling 22.9 percent.

Unfortunately dropping out perpetuates poverty because dropouts typically earn $10,000 less per year than high school graduates according to The American Academy. What is absolutely predictable is that many high school dropouts who chose not to finish high school do poorly in life.

Another thing that may hold you back from "doing well in school" is allowing distractions, maybe you allow your friends to stop you from studying, or you are preoccupied with a girlfriend or boyfriend. What ever the reasons you may have for dropping out of school. I hope that you will take this books information very seriously. It is not a good idea to Quit on your future success and the things that must be done for you to get there. Some of our youth do not believe that a high school diploma can get them anywhere in life. They hang around their peers that have the same thinking, so this kind of thinking becomes what you believe. The vast majority of youth in the world finish high school but not in the United States. More than a million young people drop out every year, around 7,000 a day, and the numbers are rising. I have written this book in an effort to make a difference in the lives of teens.

I want to help prevent at-risk youth from short-circuiting their futures by inspiring them to stay in school and graduate. I have a chant I use when speaking to high school students. I teach it to them and I say what ever high school name it is" Are you with me. They will yell "oh Yeah we are committed to graduate. I say are you with me, and the again will yell "Oh Yeah we are committed to graduate. Are you committed to graduating high school, if not make the commitment today.

# Chapter 3

# Graduation Day

## Why is it important to graduate high school

High school can be difficult, but it is an important stepping stone into the adult world. A high school diploma gives you opportunities to continue your education and the potential to earn more income. If you don't enjoy high school and dread attending classes each day, you might be wondering what could be so bad about dropping out. There are many reasons why you should stay in school until graduation day. Graduating from high school will help boost your confidence and self-esteem.

Young people without a high school diploma are four times as likely to be unemployed as those who complete at least four years of college, according to the National Dropout Prevention Center. Most all jobs that pay more than minimum wage require a high school diploma. With a high school diploma or a college or technical degree, you're more likely to receive a job that provides higher wages as well as health insurance and retirement benefits. A high school diploma also offers more lifetime opportunities outside of the job sector. You're more likely to live above the poverty line, which means you'll be able to apply for loans to buy a home or pay for higher education.

Graduating high school gives you the chance to learn a variety of things. The more you learn the better off you will be. High school will be worth while if you learn. High school will be worth while if you stay. Every Student should commit to finishing school and, incidentally, I encourage everyone to do exactly that, but understand something" you will never finish your education. You can make school easy; but that's not true with education. Many times it's very difficult and it is a lifetime project. We all should commit to life long learning and education. Commitment, persistence, and a plan of action will provide you with the education you so desperately need to climb much higher on the success ladder in life. The message I'm communicating should be quite clear: Don't let a lack of schooling be an excuse for not getting an education. I can assure you it will affect your personal life, your family life and your career. So, get that education. You must take your education seriously because it is preparing you for the market place. My mentor Jim Rohn taught me that economics is simple we all get paid for bringing value to the market place. It takes time to bring value to the market place. However we don't get paid for time. Someone may say I am making 20 dollars per hour, that's really not true. Because if that were true you could just stay home. Then just have them send you your money. We don't get paid for time we get paid for value we bring to the market place. Is it possible to become twice as valuable to the market place to earn twice as much money? The answer is YES. You could become three times as valuable. Why would someone in the market place pay someone just $5.00 per hour. The answer is simple they are not very valuable. To become more valuable to the market place you must work harder on yourself than you do on your job. If you would change then things will change for you.

You won't be as likely to need public assistance, with a High school diploma. Graduating from high school will determine how well you live for the next 50 years of your life. Society respects and desires people who are well educated and knowledgeable.

So by now you should know that putting in the time now to finish school and receive your high school diploma is likely to have a positive effect on future educational opportunities, job options and earning potential. Think seriously before you consider dropping out. For without a high school diploma, many educational and professional opportunities will not be available to you. While some employers may hire you without a high school diploma, you're unlikely to be promoted and may never find yourself reaching the management level. If you want to move on to a higher education, colleges and universities look more favorably on prospective students who have attained a high school diploma indicating the satisfactory completion of a general education throughout high school. High school graduates are positive role models, obtaining a high school diploma is an honored achievement! More and more employers prefer to hire someone who has an education. A high school education can help prepare a student to enter the workplace, which is why employers value a high school diploma. The students who have chosen to dropout might not realize just how much having or not having a high school diploma can affect their future lives. A high school diploma shows the employer that you do have an educational background and other skills, such as problem solving, that you've obtained through your classes. If you are considering not earning your diploma, After you have finished reading this book make a list of the benefits of dropping out of school, and then one considering the benefits of earning your diploma. Compare the two and then decide. Think hard about your decision before leaving high school it's much easier to leave than to return. The sad fact is that Two-fifths of high school students who graduate are prepared neither for traditional college nor for career training, according to a study from researchers at Johns Hopkins University and the University of Arizona. It is absolutely vital that every student take their education seriously and get all the information that you can while you are in school. Remember everything that you will accomplish in life will come from Education,Training and your own Personal Development. Let me explain why? Once you have been educated you will now move on to the market place where you will be trained to do the job.

Now once you have been trained to do the job, now come personal development. Here you must work harder on yourself than you do on anything else. Why? to make yourself more valuable to the market place. Your life depends on your commitment to getting an education. Do your dead level best to get it all, because there is nothing worse than being stupid. Political correctness aside, most people who don't graduate from high school may not be able to achieve their dreams. Profile a decent sized group of individuals who dropped out of high school and ask yourself, "Do I want to be like them in 10 years?" In addition to dropouts the most common group among non high school graduates there are those who don't score necessarily well on state proficiency exams. In other words, they attended high school but didn't learn anything.

Regardless of the reasons behind not passing minimum skills tests of graduation, these students, too, struggle for success. So whatever it is that's holding a student back, he or she needs to find a way to compensate for their weakness as opposed to making excuses or they, too, will end up near the bottom portion of society.

Many students have experienced the over whelming excitement as they approach high school graduation day. I can remember feeling anxious to celebrate the big day with my friends and family, while at the same time I was panicking thinking about having to walk across the stage in front of that many people. Then, the more I thought about the reality of graduation day, I started to get curious, but nervous, about being able to start a new chapter in my life once graduation day had passed. If I were back in high school and someone asked about my plans for the future, I'd say that my first priority was to learn what the options were. You don't need to be in a rush to choose your life's work. What you need to do is discover what you are passionate about. You have to work on stuff you like if you want to be good at what you do. Most people like to be good at what they do. In the so-called real world this need is a powerful force. But high school students rarely benefit from it.

Why? Because when your in high school, you must let yourself believe that your job is to be a high school student. And so you let yourself think that you need to be good at what you do by being satisfied merely for doing well in school. If you'd asked me in high school what the difference was between high school kids and adults, I'd have said it was that adults had to earn a living. I later found out that this is wrong. Adults take responsibility for themselves. Making a living is only a small part of the process. It's far more important to take intellectual responsibility for yourself. If I had to go through high school again, I'd treat it like a job. During this time of my life I would focus solely on becoming the best student of learning I could become. When I you ask students what they regret most about high school, they nearly all say the same thing that they wasted to much time. You may be thinking, we have to do more than get good grades. We have to have extracurricular activities. Extracurricular activities are not getting things done. I am not saying that you shouldn't be involved in extracurricular activities, what I am saying is you must treat going to school like your life depended on your learning the things that you are taught. What you should not do is rebel and decide to check out and quit school. Most students think they hate math, but the boring stuff you do in school under the name "mathematics" is not at all like what mathematicians do. The great mathematician G. H. Hardy said he didn't like math in high school either. He only took it up because he was better at it than the other students. Only later did he realize math was interesting only later did he start to ask questions instead of merely answering them correctly. Asking questions moves you to a higher ground of learning what you really want to know. Why? because you really want to know. You may ask if it takes years to articulate great questions, what do you do now, at sixteen? Work toward finding one. Great questions don't appear suddenly. Don't disregard unseemly motivations. One of the most powerful is the desire to be better than other people at something. Hardy said that's what got him started, and I think the only unusual thing about him is that he admitted it. Another powerful motivator is the desire to do, or know, things you're not supposed to. Do everything you possible to increase your learning. Dare to believe in yourself and what you can truly accomplish and decide to make it your best year ever. Remember a wise student will increase their learning. This learning will serve you very well in life.

# Chapter 4

## Think Again Before Dropping Out

It's never to late to get back on track

Kathy said that she didn't really care her freshman year in high school. She felt that hey I'm just a freshman and thought just have fun. I have three years to catch up with my grades so it was just like a little party life for me. I kept getting F's on my report cards. I wasn't passing anything. "The problem with Kathy was she wasn't going to school she was only in school 2 to 3 days a week." The over all year I had 50 to 60 absences. I just found out that my mom had been diagnosed with a brain tumor. When I thought about a brain tumor I thought I only had a little time left with my mom. I would say there is no point I am not doing anything. I'm not going to do any work I'm not going to learn this is going to be on my mind so I just never would. Ray said that one of his teachers had a long talk with him. She told him that she would work with him. Ray said that he really didn't want to get a GED he wanted some type of help because he wanted to change and graduate and get out of there and get on with his life. Any help that I can get I'll take it a second chance is good enough for me and I took the second chance. According to a study done by the US. Dept of education the number one reason teens dropout of High School is a lack of involvement from their parents, and a lack of encouragement from their teachers. Out of the 5000 teenagers polled 75% sited that a lack of support was their reason for dropping out. Studies show that students who dropout of high school face an up hill battle for the rest of their lives. Your chances of ending up with a low paying job or no job at all is extremely high. Some of them will have to rely on government supported programs to survive. Which not only affects their quality of life but affects our national economy as a whole. According to a national study endorsed by law enforcement officers from around the country. Dropouts are 3 and 1/2 times more likely to commit a crime and 8 times as likely to be Incarcerated than someone who graduates high school. Studies also show that by Increasing graduation rates by just 10% prevents 3000 murders, 175,000 aggravated assaults in this country each year. I don't have no family to support me for real said Rashad. I don't got no body to support me. 17 year old Rashad wishes everyday that he would have stayed in school and finished.

Rashad made good grades but had a temper. So instead of graduating with his class mates he will spend the next 53 years behind bars. For Rashad things went from bad to worse. He was expelled from school for three months. While having free time at home he joined a gang and he was only 15 years old at the time.

It was not long Rashad was convicted of robbery and criminal activity. His 45 years sentence was suspended but now he is a convicted felon and on probation. Rashad returned home and with in one year he was arrested again. This time he received 25 years for probation violation and another 28 years for malicious wounding and possession of a firearm by a convicted felon. Rashad regrets his decision to get caught up in crime and said that he could have been a great athlete for he was once running track. Getting in trouble at school lead to dropping out of High school and he had to survive some how so he turned to crime. Like a high percentage of the dropouts in America he to ended up in prison. He now realizes that the things he was doing was stupid. You may ask when it comes to going to school what's the point in being here. Why should I listen to the teacher? What does this lesson have to do with my life? I understand that students deal with questions before and after dropping out. Questions like should I dropout of school? Did I mess up to bad? Is it to late for me to go back to finish school? I think that once students understand there is a road that you can travel and still have an opportunity to finish what you started and graduate high school. Many students across the country have done it. You can still go back to your high school and get your diploma. Never let your friends be more important than your education you have got to think about your future and how you are going to live and eat. You cannot give up on yourself go back to school and if your already in school stay there until you finish and graduate. When you learn that your freedom is actually connected to your education, where you can now support yourself. You can go and do and accomplish what ever you want to accomplish. If and when you can realize that as a dropout you can go back to school. Then use your education as a tool to get your life back on track. I get the fact that most young people want to belong to something. Whether it's a club or team or a certain group of students. Whether you belong or you don't belong is important I know. Because if you don't belong you will find something to belong and it may not be a positive move for you. If it is negative it could be your down fall to wanted to dropout of school. I want every student in America to understand that you are all VIP's in this case it means Very Important People. You have Greatness in you and you are valuable. Now you must develop that Greatness through education first. If a student dropouts it does not mean that they are a bad person. I know that life happens to all of us and there can be circumstances that you find yourselves in that can contribute to your dropping out of school. Sometimes our personal lives get in the way of things we want to accomplish. I say if that happens do not give up on your dreams and your future success. Go back to school and get what you went there to get in the first place. A High School Diploma is the beginning of your life going into the market place to go to work. It's never to late to go back to school if you need to. Daniel Paris, a young man who was identified to have multiple learning disabilities, as well as attention deficit hyperactivity disorder (ADHD). After dropping out of high school during sophomore year, Daniel returned to school and completed his degree. He's now a graduate student at Harvard University. Not only did he graduate from college, he graduated from Harvard with honors. He wrote a book in which he boldly tells his story and offers up inspiration to others who might be in the same situation. While high school dropout percentages in the U.S. are much lower today than they were a few decades ago, there is still a lot of room for improvement. Richard Carmona dropped out of school at age 16 to join the Army after going through everything from being homeless to having health problems when he was young. He's definitely a high school dropout who went on to do amazing things because he earned his GED and traveled a road that led him to be the 17th Surgeon General in the history of the U.S. He served 4 years in that position. After his GED, he went on to be a decorated Special Forces Vietnam Vet and then went on to college after he finished his active status. He went on to get an associate of art degree and didn't stop there. He eventually furthered his studies all the way to getting a medical degree and earned status as the top rated graduate of his class. You'll be competing for jobs your whole life, and your education is the only thing that gives you an edge when you're young and don't have much work experience. Many employers will screen you out entirely because you have no degree despite your experience. They'll nearly always take someone with a high school degree over someone without.

More and more, an education is becoming mandatory in our economy. Some teenage dropouts believe they'll always be able to ask others for help when they need it, so they don't need a degree and a well-paying job. But minimum wage isn't enough to support basic needs in most areas of the country, and your parents and friends won't always be able to help you support yourself. Once you get older, the kind of help you expected as a teenager will dry up and people will expect you to take care of yourself. Even when you get a job, your level of education may hold you back. As the least educated on your team, you could be among the first to go when your company needs to lay off employees. You will have a harder time moving forward in your career without a degree. And once you lose a job, it will be harder to get a new one. High school dropouts are definitely the most vulnerable to losing income and staying in low income brackets in our society. You will be competing against high school and college grads all your life if you become a high school dropout. Why would anyone give up a chance to learn for a life of struggle. More than half the students who dropout do so by the tenth grade. 20% dropout by the eighth grade, and 3% dropout by the fourth grade. Not all teenagers think before they act. 34% of young women give up on their education and dropout of school. High School dropouts are 72% more likely to be unemployed compared to high school graduates. Young people you have got to understand this is your life. One of the powerful solutions for living an extraordinary life would be to get a good education and learn all you can. Listen to what these students said about dropping out and going back to school.

After I made some bad choices during the first few months in my first year of high school, I was removed and placed in a place (which was more akin to a Juvenile Detention Camp than an actual school). Leaving high school in the first place was the greatest mistake of my life and it lead me onto a path that I never wanted to take and I paid the price for it. But now I'm going back to school to finish my education and get my diploma. -Emily

My freshman year when I was 15 I got pregnant and had an abortion. ( I was forced to because I was a minor). I had to

work also to support myself because my parents barley made any money to even pay the bills, So i started working at 16. I made straight A's with a gpa of 4.03999 until second semester of junior year, at 17 I was to worn down from working and tried online school threw the county to get my high school diploma. online school ended up not working for me.
I recently took my GED this year in May and PASSED!! I'm 18 years old turning 19. So I went up to a community college the very next day and applied. I now start college this month :). I will be working towards getting into the nursing program. -Mandy

To be honest, I dropped out of school in about 8th grade. Since then I haven't continued my education at all which has in a lot of ways corrupted the education that I already had due to lack of brain use. I was locked up for a couple years and it wasted a lot of my time. Yes, I'm aware that I did this too myself. When I got out I was left with no one, and still have no one. I need to go back and learn the basics of things, starting at a community college and slowly working up. I'm just curious if this 5 year break from education academically and lack of life experience has crippled my chances of ever making something out of myself. I'm 18 by the way and a very lonely teen at that with no direction. I'm trying to make a plan to get my life started again, but my biggest fear is that I'll never Truly be able to recover because of my lost time. I've been a recluse for 2 years and there's just things that I should know in society and other aspects of life, but I don't. I try to go out and start my life, but I struggle with things now that people have learned when they were kids and I get so frustrated with myself. I see all these people around and it's so depressing because it only reminds me of my mistakes, what I would've been, and that I can't relate to ANY of my peers. Now that I'm interested in getting an education, it seems pointless. I can't seem to get myself out of this huge hole I put myself in, and IF I ever get out, it'll be to late. I'm so lonely and it's almost impossible to find someone to experience life with now because I'm so far behind. I will always be the under dog. -Anonymus

I'm 28 years old and had to leave high school because of economic reasons. Now that I'm more stable and just got my GED, I'm preparing myself for the SAT exam. Will I still be able to be accepted by a college? I'm a bit nervous because I know my transcript are not great. I want to go to FIU to get my undergraduate degree, and then I want to go to a veterinary school. Thank you in advance for any advice you can give me to improve my chances of admission. -Anonymus

It is a really a bad idea to dropout of school because things are bad at school because you are being harassed (sexually or otherwise) or bullied try changing schools rather than quitting. It is so not worth it - if academics are hard for you see your school counselor about a non-academic program, voluntarily set yourself back a grade, or get Learning Assistance (even if it is informally from a friend). Drop outs have a harder time getting good, secure, decent paying jobs. More and more entry level and trade specific jobs require a minimum of high school graduation. Dropping out gives you a lot of free time, even if you get a full time job, you are more likely to get in to a self destructive things like drugs and/or alcohol, gangs and criminal activity. Pregnancy is not a good reason to drop out and get a job, look in to your options before taking such a drastic step (many schools and communities have programs designed to keep teens with children in school). Being a drop out is much harder than you think it will be. Going back to school as an adult is not as easy as you think it will be, and often costs you money high school is free. Dropping out is not cool, it does not make you smart, nor does it mean you are grown up or more mature in fact it makes you the exact opposite of all these things. If you are a High School dropout It's time to erase "high school dropout" from your record and start over with a clean slate. Because it's never too late to go back to school.

# Chapter 5

# You Must Create a Plan for Yourself

## Planning and Decision Making

Without planning you will run into more difficult problems in preparing to finish school and graduate. Planning is an essential part of almost every short-term goal and long-term goal, or future endeavor. Getting a good education is the bridge between where you are now and where you will be in the real world. It is vital that you invest some time in planning for your future. You must discover who you are by finding your interest your strengths and your values. You have to also know the options that you have ahead of you. What are you interested in doing with your life. Perhaps it's business, Art, engineer, Doctor, Lawyer, Judge. Now at this point you must make a decision to what it is you will need to do to further your education to tap into the field that you would like to be a part of. You may want to go to college but how you perform in high school lets College Universities gauge what type of student you are. The decisions that you will make in the years you are in High School will determine where you end up. Whether you are facing a problem, trying to sort out your life, or simply want to structure your day, you are going to need a plan. First if you don't know where you're going, you're likely to wind up anywhere. Creating a powerful a plan always begins with having a clear purpose, vision or goal in mind. In fact, the plan is designed to take you from wherever you are right now directly to the accomplishment of your stated goal (Graduation Day)". The point of creating a good plan is to give you, more tangible goals and targets to work towards. This way, it's easier to stay focused and to be encouraged by results you can measure and see. By setting a goal to graduate it's going to take focus. Have you thought about what you want to be doing in the next five years? Do you know what you want to achieve by the end of today?

If you want to succeed, you need to set goals. Without goals you lack focus and direction. Goal setting not only allows you to take control of your life's direction; it also provides you a place for determining whether you are actually succeeding. To accomplish your goals, however, you need to know how to set them. You can't simply say, "I want" and expect it to happen. Goal setting is a process that starts with careful consideration of what you want to achieve, and ends with a lot of hard work and dedication to actually get the job done. When you set goals for yourself, it is important that they motivate you: this means making sure that they are important to you, and that there is value in achieving them. I promise you that finishing school and receiving your high school diploma is important. If you have little interest in Graduating, then the chances of you putting in the work to make it happen are slim.

Your being Motivated is key to achieving your goals. Goal achievement requires commitment, so to maximize the likelihood of success, you need to feel a sense of urgency and have an "I must do this" attitude. When you don't have this attitude, you risk putting off what you need to do to make the goal of graduating a reality. To make sure your goal is motivating, write down why it's valuable and important to you. Ask yourself, "If I were to share my goal with others, what would I tell them to convince them it was a worthwhile goal?" You can use this motivating value statement to help you if you start to doubt yourself or lose confidence in your ability to actually make the goal happen. Goal setting is much more than simply saying you want something to happen. Unless you clearly define exactly what you want and understand why you want it in the first place, the odds of success are considerably reduced. Here are some pointers in keeping up with your homework for starters.

With a little organization and discipline, you can get all of your homework done on time, every day. Develop a plan that will break down your homework tasks into smaller and manageable units. Write your assignments down accurately and promptly when they are given. You cannot plan your homework time effectively if you do not know exactly what to do. Estimate how much time will be needed to complete each assignment. Be realistic. It is better to carve out more time than less. If you finish early, you can use your bonus time for another subject. Remember that if you have extra time left over, you can reward yourself by doing something other than homework. Decide how much time you have available for homework after school for each day of the week. For example, Monday - 1 hour, Tuesday - 1 1/2 hours, Wednesday - 1/2 hour, etc. On days where you have other planned activities, whether it's an extracurricular activity or chores or quality time with your family, you will have less time for homework. Break down your homework time. Look at your assignments and consider how much time you need to devote to each. Find time in your homework schedule to get it done, preferably a day early. If you have a five-page Math paper due on Friday, evenly spread the total amount of hours you believe it is going to take to complete the paper between each day. Write in break times.

This will stop you from getting too overwhelmed and frustrated during long stretches of homework time and will help you to keep your mind focused. A ten-minute break for each hour of homework done is a good guideline. Use this time to stretch, wash your face, walk around the block, unload the dishwasher for your parents, get something to drink, or do anything that won't tempt you to delay your return to homework. Do not extend the time you take to for your breaks. Certainly don't start goofing off. Stick with the schedule. Once you have your schedule, follow it, or else all the planning in the world is useless. Your plans won't work if you won't work. Avoid distractions such as TV, video games, phone conversation, or surfing the internet. You must fully devote your schedule to doing this. That means turning off all electronics except your lamp, clock, and room light, and, if needed, your computer. You may even want to turn off your phone.

If you find your energy drops quickly, do the hardest subject first, when your energy is highest.

After that is done, everything else will feel like going downhill. When scheduling, do not forget to write down time you cannot be doing homework, like when you are at sports practice, or babysitting. If you find that you do not have enough time to get all your homework done, look for more time that you can devote to homework by replacing other regular activities. Instead of spending an hour chatting on the computer with your friends, for instance, limit yourself strictly to fifteen or twenty minutes. However, if you are still struggling even after you have devoted every available minute to homework, talk to your parents or your teacher about it. The key here is to help keep you focused on where it is your going with your life. The habits that you create in high school will follow you directly into the work place. Planning takes just a little bit of effort on your part. By creating a plan for success in school you give yourself a means for that success. I want you to understand that while many people consider college as preparation for the real world, the decisions made during high school can have the biggest impact on your career success. The problem for many students, and even parents, is that they fail to think of high-school education as a good investment. A free high-school education will cost taxpayers on an average of about $40,000 over four years. The success gap in the market place between those who choose to finish high school and those who drop out is huge and has risen sharply over time."

Students who pay close attention to the decisions made in

high school from elective courses to after-school activities will find that it helps them in not only their pursuit of postsecondary education but in their pursuit of a fulfilling career. So I say take the time to plan well, while you are in high school and don't wait til college to do so. For some of you may not go to college but will still have to be prepared to move into the market place.

Preparation is never wasted time. You've got This!!!!! Let me tell you something about Goals. There's no telling what you can do when you get inspired by them. There's no telling what you can do when you believe in them. And there's no telling what will happen when you act upon them. Like a well-defined dream, well-defined goals work like magnets. They pull you in their direction. The better you define them, the better you describe them, the harder you work on achieving them, the stronger they pull. Everything you need for your better future and success has already been written. And guess what? It's all available. Learning is the beginning of wealth. Learning is the beginning of spirituality. Learning is where the miracle process all begins. High school will be worthwhile if you try. Try to make some progress. Try your best. Give it every effort. High school will be worthwhile if you simply stay and see it through don't end it at the beginning nor the middle. High school will be worthwhile if you care.

If you care at all, you will get results. If you care enough, you will get incredible results. High school is worthwhile if you plan. If you don't design your own plan, chances are you'll fall into someone else's plan. High school is worthwhile if you be. Wherever you are, be there. Develop a unique focus on the current moment your in. Let others lead small lives, but not you. Let others argue over small things, but not you. Let others cry over small hurts, but not you. Let others leave their futures in someone else's hand but not You! Start by Graduating with your class. Just decide and take responsibility for doing what you need to do to insure your making exceptional progress today.

# Chapter 6

# The Value of Learning

## We are Affected by what we know

Dr. Martin Luther King Jr. said that The function of education is to teach one to think intensively and to think critically.
Intelligence plus character that is the goal of true education. Those who achieve don't do it by accident. It's a matter of studying first and practicing second. Recent research indicates that higher education is extremely valuable. A belief in equal opportunity, in education, in human dignity and hope. This epitomizes the statement the mind is a terrible thing to waste. Some of the most brilliant minds have built societies to what they are today, figured out how to eradicate some of the most horrifying diseases, solved some of the most complex math and engineering problems out there, and made leaps and bounds in ways that we communicate with each other and are entertained, to name a few. Let's just say that if you didn't use your mind, what would be the point of having one? It's like have a million dollars in the bank, but never spending it. Wouldn't that be a waste of even having it?
But what I am talking about here is it's a shame for someone with bright potential not to receive an education that could fulfill their possibilities. Most people do not realize just how important our minds are. The mind is a powerful tool. Our

minds are the reason behind innovations and inventions and it is only up to us whether we'd like to tap into its full potential or not. You have the power to do things so far beyond what you can even imagine right now. Unfortunately, because some people don't understand how their minds and thoughts in their mind work, they struggle in life. In so doing, they limit themselves and their success in life. What you allow into your mind by what you watch, listen to, read, will determine what you think. What you think will determine what you believe. What you believe will determine your philosophy. Your philosophy will determine your attitude. Your attitude will determine your actions. Your actions will determine your life and the way that life turns out. In other words these things shape your world and the way you see it. So your friends can see the world drastically different than you do. Why? The things that they allow into their minds may be different from what you allow into yours. If you have been told all your life that you are not going to amount to anything, if you hear it long enough you will believe it. Once you believe it only then will it have power over you. Once it has power over you then you see yourself not amounting to anything so it causes you to think whats the use. Listening to negative things from others without believing in yourself, to the point where you believe what they say will have a major negative impact on you and your life. Learn how to cultivate positive mindsets by reading and watching and listening to things that will make you better as a person and a student. Its said that we only use a small portion of our brains. What do you think could be achieved if we used our brain to its fullest potential? Some people go through life with their minds free wheeling which means to take no thought at all. Have you ever thought about how others shape your life? Never under estimate the power of influence. The influence of those around us is so powerful, so subtle, and so gradual that often we don't even realize how it can affect us. Don't join the easy crowd of classmates you won't grow. Go where the expectations and demands to perform are high. Keep the negative influences from your life. Teens are facing a lot of pressure today. They are surrounded by negative influences that come from all different sources: media, television, music, and the internet. Seventy-five percent of teens try alcohol before they graduate from high school, according to the "Archives of Pediatrics & Adolescent Medicine." Those who start drinking at a young age are more likely to suffer from illnesses, injure themselves or have to deal with alcohol abuse as adults. School failure alot of the time is associated with drug and alcohol use. These substances affect the mind and behavior. Teens are spending more and more time online, usually on a social media platform like Facebook or Twitter, and their online life is not just staying on their computer at home. Most teens now have smart phones where they are on social media networks all throughout the day. They are constantly texting, tweeting, and posting pictures via Snapchat and Instagram. The problem with this is teens don't know how to disconnect from all this activity. This too will affect your mind and behavior from studying and doing your homework for school. While many teens seem unconcerned about poor grades, others work hard at improving their test scores. These students realize that studying hard and doing well in school can only brighten a teen's future. Dedicating time to studying and doing homework are important parts of success in high school. Make school a priority and put school work and studying above social activities or your after school job. Being successful in high school comes with a lot of patience as well as motivation. Unfortunately there are so many distractions coming your way, sometimes it becomes hard to say no. However, if you want to become a successful student, then you have to start learning how to say no to these distractions. Another thing that will help as you are in school is to get enough sleep. Your sleep schedule can also make a big difference in how well you do in school. According to the National Sleep Foundation, teens need between 8.5 and 9.25 hours of sleep each night, but only about 15 percent of teens get this amount of sleep.

Students typically begin each new school year with a mixture of anticipation and anxiety. Will their teachers be supportive or severe? Will they succeed or not? Adding to the anxiety is the fear of public embarrassment if they do have difficulty. Now is the time to take responsiblity for your learning and your life. Learn ways to combat negative habits because the habits you form in high school will be the same habits you take with you into the real world. When attending high school, you will be educated by a teacher through giving you more knowledge not only from text books but also from teacher's experiences, training you how to improve your skill in learning.

What are Study Skills? Study skills are the skills you need to enable you to study and learn efficiently they are an important set of transferable life skills.

You will develop your own personal approach to studying and learning in a way that meets your own individual needs. As you develop your study skills you will discover what works for you, and what doesn't. You need to practise and develop your study skills. This will increase your awareness of how you study and you'll become more confident. Once mastered, study skills will be beneficial throughout your life. Many students think that being a good student means just showing up for classes, taking a few notes, reading the textbooks, and studying right before the tests.

However, learning, like many other activities, involves a complex set of skills that require practice. Studying involves learning a set of skills, such as note taking, test taking, etc., that must be practiced in order for you to become a good student. Learning how to prioritize material when studying for a test; preparing for a test over a number of days and not just the night before is essential. Ask yourself questions while you read or study. Answering them will help to make sense of the material, and aid you in remembering it, because the process will make an impression on you. When you don't know what to do when you have to study for something. Don't give up and quit go talk to someone about it; don't just keep it to yourself. never be afraid to ask for help. The easiest things to learn are things that you are interested in. Become interested in the things that you struggle with most. Education is the acquisition of knowledge.

It is taking ownership of the information given to you whether through formal education or through life skills. Formal learning is learning that takes place within a teacher-student relationship, such as in a school system. The term formal learning has nothing to do with the formality of the learning, but rather the way it is directed and organized. In formal learning, the learning or training departments set out the goals and objectives of the learning. Active learning occurs when a person takes control of their learning experience. Since understanding information is the key aspect of learning, it is important for learners to recognize what they understand and what they do not. Education can be viewed as the means by which you prepare yourself to face the modern world and survive within it. As students gains knowledge in different subjects and specializes in certain fields, he/she also grows psychologically as a person. Whether you like it or not both formal and informal education is necessary for what we learn is what we use to lead our lives to survive.

# Chapter 7

## Finish What You've Started

### Your future depends on it

I was age 45 when I heard a man in whom I consider one of my mentors the great late Mr. Jim Rohn say that, most people spend more time planning their vacation than they do their own life. I made the comittment that day to live my life on purpose. How? Intentionally and by design.
I found out that I could design the life that I wanted and was well able to pull that life off. I simply had to take all of the necessary steps for doing so. Everyone in this world should make measurable progress in reasonable time.
Progress in school, business, relationships, family, finances, spirituality, knowledge, experience, understanding and much much more. The real problem is that most people in life go year after year not making much change. Why? because they simply refuse to do whats necessary to make continual progress. You should not be in the same place next year as you were the previous year. How long should a student who is in the ninth grade stay there. I am sure you would say one year right." No one wants to go back to the ninth grade year after year for it means they are not making any progress at all. There is one thing I know and have learned and that is this. If you don't produce you won't be happy. If you can't be happy then what else is there.
If you can do better in school and life shouldn't you. In order to live up to your full potential and go on to live an

extraordinary effective life you will have to learn to finish what you've started. You must start with a plan. It's like a being builder of a house. In order to build a house you must first have a plan for what you want the house to look like. Without the plan the house cannot be built. Now if you try to build a house without a plan, it won't be much of a house and it will be very difficult to even get started. Your life is alot like building a house. You will first have to have a plan for what you want your life to look like. You will really have to set some goals for what you want to achieve and you must write those goals down. Once you have written those goals down, you have created the plan from which your life will be built. With hard work and dedication your plan can be something you see come to pass in your own life. Do you have a habit of starting projects, but not finishing them? If so, you are not alone. Many people have a habit of starting projects but not finishing them, which is a very bad practice. Completing school successfully takes proper planning and conscious action. Once you start, commit to it. Tracking your progress helps you understand how you're doing and gives you a target to reach (Graduation). This makes it easier to keep up with your momentum. The way to achieve true inner peace is to finish what you start. If you don't enjoy high school and dread going to classes each day, you might be wondering what could be so bad about dropping out. There are many reasons why you should stay in school until graduation day. Weighing these advantages against the numerous disadvantages of not earning a diploma might motivate you to stay and finish. A high school diploma offers more lifetime opportunities outside of the job sector. You're more likely to live above the poverty line, which means you'll be able to apply for loans to buy a home or pay for higher education. You won't be as likely to need public assistance, either. With a high school diploma, you're more likely to live in a neighborhood with a low crime rate and to stay out of trouble with the law yourself. Graduating from high school will help boost your confidence and self-esteem. It also helps protect your physical health, because you're more likely to have access to medical care and have the funds to pay for it.

When you graduate, you're also a role model to younger siblings, other relatives and friends, and that might encourage them to stay in school. Finishing high school gives you the chance to learn a variety of things.

The more you learn, the more well-rounded you'll be. High school teaches students more than just the basics of reading, math and science. Students also learn study skills, time management, communication and basic manners. These skills can serve students well in a variety of careers, and students who drop out may not master these skills.

You'll also increase the odds of discovering something you're passionate enough about to dedicate your life to. Your high school diploma symbolizes the fact that you have finished your high school education.

Once you have graduated, as if the teenage years aren't stressful enough, you must consider what to do now that you have a high school diploma. You will have plenty of options to choose from. You could choose to jump right in and join the ranks of the workforce. Unfortunately, many right-out-of-high-school jobs pay less than the ones you could get after attending college or technical school. I hope now that you can see that finishing high school is very important to your success and your future.

For things to change for any student that is not doing so well in school they will have to change. Success comes from growth; it comes from growing bigger than the problems and obstacles that surround you. Don't search for success commit to grow, commit to become, commit to do what you know to do, and you will attract success. The greatest investment you will ever make is in yourself. Work to become a better person; everyday you want to be slightly better than you were the day before. Success is the natural consequence of consistently applying the basic fundamentals that you have learned." Success is neither magical nor mysterious. Never give up. If you just keep at it, eventually you will get to where you want to be. Who are you talking to? Who are you listening to? What seeds are being planted into your life? Your environment is critical! In order for your life to produce fruit, it must be planted in the right environment. You wouldn't try to plant tomato seeds in the dessert because it's not the right environment for a tomato seed to produce. Likewise, don't try to become successful surrounded by negative people. Create an environment where you can flourish. Learn to guard what you hear; guard what gets planted in your thoughts, so you can become all that you were destined to become. Nothing happens overnight, look at anyone who's successful. It's taken them years to get there, sometimes decades, don't think you are any different. If it took them years, don't be surprised when it takes you years.

In other words, manage your expectations, so you don't get disappointed unnecessarily. Success is possible, but it won't happen tomorrow, if you just began today. Remember, success is not a single event; you don't become a success in a moment. Success comes from moving in the right direction every day for years. Your education is the beginning of those years of preparation for successful living. Now if you will set your mind on what you want to accomplish. It's not the circumstances of life that determine where you end up, it's your commitment to arrive at your intended destination that determines your success. Time is something that I had to learn to value and so will you. There is nothing more valuable than time. You can sow your time and get anything you want. You can sow your time and get more friends, more money, or better health. Nothing is more priceless than time, so never waste this precious gift called time. I've never met a rich man who didn't value his time, and I've never met a poor man who did. Learn to see the value of time because with time, anything can be accomplished! The time you spend in school learning should be valued time for you as a student. This time is not to be wasted at all, for it is time well invested for your future.

Time is more valuable than money. You can always get more money, but you cannot get more time." Slowly but surely." That's exactly how your dreams come to pass when you commit to achieve them. You simply have to never quit. Consider the ant, if he is stopped he continues to look for another way to go. How long will the ant look? He will look and search until he finds it or until he dies. What I am trying to say here is stay in school and finish what you have started. Why? because quitting cannot become an option for you to take if you want to experience success in your life. Once you become a quitter you will continue on quitting and quitting so much so that you will hardly accomplish anything at all. Are You Going to Finish Strong? Are you committed to graduate? Do you believe in yourself? What does your future look like in your own mind? I happen to believe that by adopting the Finish Strong Attitude you can achieve breakthroughs throughout your high school years that will send you directly toward the successful future you desire. Only you have the power to choose how to respond to the challenges you face everyday in school. How will you choose to respond? Will you lie down or will you choose to fight? The choice is yours and I challenge you to always choose to Finish Strong. "It's not what happens to you that matters, it's how you choose to respond that matters. Now get up and go finish what you have started for there is Greatness in you. "Now go develop that Greatness, starting by graduating with your class! I say CONGRATULATIONS! in advance.

38110152R00029

Made in the USA
Middletown, DE
12 December 2016